CAPTURING GOD

THE SURPRISING IMAGE
THAT REVEALS THE TRUTH
ABOUT GOD

RICO TICE

TRUTH FOR LIFE®

THE BIBLE-TEACHING MINISTRY OF **ALISTAIR BEGG**

The mission of Truth For Life is to teach the Bible with clarity and relevance so that unbelievers will be converted, believers will be established, and local churches will be strengthened.

Daily Program

Each day, Truth For Life distributes the Bible teaching of Alistair Begg across the U.S., and in several locations outside of the U.S. on over 1,600 radio outlets. To find a radio station near you, visit **truthforlife.org/station-finder.**

Free Teaching

The daily program, and Truth For Life's entire teaching archive of over 2,000 Bible-teaching messages, can be accessed for free online and through Truth For Life's full-feature mobile app. A daily app is also available that provides direct access to the daily message and daily devotional. Download the free mobile apps at **truthforlife.org/app** and listen free online at **truthforlife.org.**

At-Cost Resources

Books and full-length teaching from Alistair Begg on CD, DVD and MP3CD are available for purchase at cost, with no mark up. Visit **truthforlife.org/store**.

Where To Begin?

If you're new to Truth For Life and would like to know where to begin listening and learning, find starting point suggestions at **truthforlife.org/firststep**. For a full list of ways to connect with Truth For Life, visit **truthforlife.org/subscribe.**

Contact Truth For Life

P.O. Box 398000 Cleveland, Ohio 44139
phone 1 (888) 588-7884   **email** letters@truthforlife.org
 /truthforlife   @truthforlife   truthforlife.org

Capturing God
© Rico Tice/The Good Book Company, 2017

Published by
The Good Book Company
Tel (UK): 0333 123 0880
Tel (North America): (1) 866 244 2165
International: +44 (0) 208 942 0880
Email (UK): info@thegoodbook.co.uk
Email (North America): info@thegoodbook.com

Websites
UK & Europe: www.thegoodbook.co.uk
North America: www.thegoodbook.com
Australia: www.thegoodbook.com.au
New Zealand: www.thegoodbook.co.nz

Printed and bound by CPI Group (UK) Ltd, Croydon, CR0 4YY

Design by André Parker

CONTENTS

1. A picture paints   5
2. Integrity   15
3. Welcome   27
4. Justice   39
5. Peace   49
6. Finding yourself   57

To George Tice,
my older brother and best man

┌1┐
A PICTURE PAINTS

For me, it's the one with my dad and my family, on a golf course in February, grinning and squinting in 40mph winds.

Dad's in a wheelchair. And it's the last time he'll visit this golf course, where he'd taught me how to play (erratically) and which had for years been the main place where we shared time together while steadfastly refusing to give each other short putts. His smile speaks of good memories.

Lucy, my wife, is holding our two-month-old baby and smiling too. She's smiling in a way that suggests she's thinking, "Rico is mad". She's there because it means a lot to me, and her presence speaks of her affection for me.

My two older kids are smiling because, well, they've been told to. The fact that the boys listened is remarkable. The fact that they are not actually looking at the camera is normal. (Why is it that children have an in-built tendency never to look at a camera?) Their expressions speak of that basic excitement about each day that young children seem to have.

And then there's me. I'm smiling, because there are three generations of Tices together and I can't quite believe I've managed to organise it, albeit in the midst of a gale. I'm scruffy because… well, I'm always scruffy (at the time, I thought I looked smart, but the camera never lies). My grin tells you a tale of a man who is scruffily content.

For me, that's the photo that captures my family. It's a mixture of memories and characteristics, of the place and the time and the moment. It's a picture I love to look at, because it somehow captures the essence of the Tices. It paints our characters; it sums us up. And when I look at it, it changes how I feel. It makes me smile.

Most of us have a photo like that of a loved one. It might be the person you married. Your best friend. A parent. Your kids. It might hang in your house or sit on a shelf or be tucked into a wallet or be the lockscreen on your smartphone. And you love it, because somehow it captures who that person is. And it makes you smile. It really changes how you feel.

You may not be particularly bothered about the Tice family or about a picture that sums us up. That's fair enough. But imagine being offered one photograph

6

that captured the essence of God. Imagine that God offered to hang in a frame an image that revealed everything that he wants to reveal about himself.

What would you expect to see? What would it be a picture of? Maybe you expect me to tell you about one of those Victorian paintings where a blond-haired, blue-eyed Jesus is chatting to some children. Or an old guy who looks a bit like your granddad, sitting on a throne. Or a bright white light and not much else. Or nothing at all.

But as you approach this frame, it contains none of those things. Instead what you see is... a barbarous execution.

This should sound bizarre—that this would be the way that God has chosen to reveal himself. That this could be the best way for God to tell you what he's like—to capture his character in a single scene.

Yet that's what the Christian message claims. And if you find that weird, you're ready to wrestle with it. If you find it normal, then let me say it again: the picture that best captures who God is is a picture of a man hanging on the most brutal instrument of torture and execution mankind has ever invented.

We're used to seeing that instrument, a cross, hanging in church buildings and round people's necks. But that's quite strange when you think about it. It's like putting an electric chair at the front of church services. The symbol at the heart of the Christian faith is not a crib to remind people of its founder's birth. It's not a lamp to point to his teaching. It's not a stone to repeat the claim that he rose from the dead.

It's a cross, to point to his death. A cross, to reach back to the events of the first Good Friday.

No other world religion celebrates the death of its founder. Christianity focuses on it. Why? Why is this symbol of universal loathing a badge of honour for Christians?

Because this is the place that best captures God. And so this is the place that this book is about. Which means it won't be poetic or full of fun—as the poet W.H. Auden once wrote, "Christmas and Easter can be subjects for poetry but Good Friday, like Auschwitz, cannot". It will surprise you. It should shock you. It may well offend you. But it might just thrill you and it might just change you, too.

For me, it's the picture with my dad and family, in the wind, on a golf course.

For God, it's the picture where a man was brutally murdered, in darkness, on a cross.

Will you look at it?

THE PICTURE

They say a picture paints a thousand words. A thousand words can paint a very good picture, too— and so, in this case, can precisely 823 words. So here's the picture. It's taken from one of the four biographies of Jesus, or "Gospels", in the Bible. This one's written by a doctor and historian called Luke. As you read it, paint the picture in your head. Read it slowly, and pause to add the detail to the scene—the sights, the sounds, the shouts, the silences.

In the next few chapters, I'm going to focus on some of the details of the picture—but first, I need you to paint it in your mind. It's about AD 33. We open with the Roman governor of Judea, a province of the Roman Empire on the eastern edge of the Mediterranean Sea. He's in Jerusalem, the capital of Judea, and he's calling together the local religious and political leaders of the conquered nation of Israel, along with a mob of ordinary residents, to announce his judgment on a man who they have accused of treason—a man named Jesus…

Pilate called together the chief priests, the rulers and the people, and said to them, "You brought me this man as one who was inciting the people to rebellion. I have examined him in your presence and have found no basis for your charges against him. Neither has Herod, for he sent him back to us; as you can see, he has done nothing to deserve death. Therefore, I will punish him and then release him."

But the whole crowd shouted, "Away with this man! Release Barabbas to us!" (Barabbas had been thrown into prison for an insurrection in the city, and for murder.)

Wanting to release Jesus, Pilate appealed to them again. But they kept shouting, "Crucify him! Crucify him!"

For the third time he spoke to them: "Why? What crime has this man committed? I have found in him no grounds for the death penalty. Therefore I will have him punished and then release him."

But with loud shouts they insistently demanded that he be crucified, and their shouts prevailed. So Pilate decided to grant their demand. He released the man who had been thrown into prison for insurrection and murder, the one they asked for, and surrendered Jesus to their will.

As the soldiers led him away, they seized Simon from Cyrene, who was on his way in from the country, and put the cross on him and made him carry it behind Jesus. A large number of people followed him, including women who mourned and wailed for him. Jesus turned and said to them, "Daughters of Jerusalem, do not weep for me; weep for yourselves and for your children. For the time will come when you will say, 'Blessed are the childless women, the wombs that never bore and the breasts that never nursed!' Then,

*'they will say to the mountains, "Fall on us!"
and to the hills, "Cover us!"'*

*For if people do these things when the tree is green,
what will happen when it is dry?"*

And so we reach the moment, the single scene, the
crucial image…

*Two other men, both criminals, were also led out
with him to be executed. When they came to the
place called the Skull, they crucified him there, along
with the criminals—one on his right, the other on his
left. Jesus said, "Father, forgive them, for they do not
know what they are doing." And they divided up his
clothes by casting lots.*

*The people stood watching, and the rulers even
sneered at him. They said, "He saved others;
let him save himself if he is God's Messiah, the
Chosen One."*

*The soldiers also came up and mocked him. They
offered him wine vinegar and said, "If you are the
king of the Jews, save yourself."*

*There was a written notice above him, which
read: THIS IS THE KING OF THE JEWS.*

*One of the criminals who hung there hurled insults at
him: "Aren't you the Messiah? Save yourself and us!"*

But the other criminal rebuked him. "Don't you fear God," he said, "since you are under the same sentence? We are punished justly, for we are getting what our deeds deserve. But this man has done nothing wrong."

Then he said, "Jesus, remember me when you come into your kingdom."

Jesus answered him, "Truly I tell you, today you will be with me in paradise."

It was now about noon, and darkness came over the whole land until three in the afternoon, for the sun stopped shining. And the curtain of the temple was torn in two. Jesus called out with a loud voice, "Father, into your hands I commit my spirit." When he had said this, he breathed his last.

The centurion, seeing what had happened, praised God and said, "Surely this was a righteous man." When all the people who had gathered to witness this sight saw what took place, they beat their breasts and went away. But all those who knew him, including the women who had followed him from Galilee, stood at a distance, watching these things.

Now there was a man named Joseph, a member of the Council, a good and upright man, who had not consented to their decision and action. He came from the Judean town of Arimathea, and he himself was waiting for the kingdom of God. Going to Pilate, he asked for Jesus' body. Then he took it down, wrapped it in linen cloth and placed it in a tomb cut in the rock, one in which no one had yet been laid. It was Preparation Day, and the Sabbath was about to begin.

The women who had come with Jesus from Galilee followed Joseph and saw the tomb and how his body was laid in it.

(Taken from the Bible, from the Gospel of Luke, chapter 23, verses 13 to 55)

2
INTEGRITY

When I was 14, I went to church voluntarily for the first time. I had a really good reason for going. She was called Emma.

Emma was very pretty, and I used to like watching her walk up and down the aisle, past where I sat. I never spoke to her, and she never spoke to me, but she's the reason I'm now a pastor—and so in a sense, if you don't like this book, she's the one who is to blame.

Anyway, I was at this service because of Emma, with not much thought of anything other than her, when the guy who was speaking at the front said the most formative thing that anyone said to me during all my years at school. He was speaking about this execution scene, and about how the man hanging on the cross, the man Jesus from Nazareth, had said as nails were driven into his hands:

Father, forgive them, for they do not know what they are doing. (Luke 23 v 34)

And the guy in that church said something like this:

"Who is this man, who, having been unjustly tried, having been deserted by his friends, having been despised and rejected by his own people, having been spat upon and flogged and scourged, having had his head crowned with thorns and then his feet nailed to a Roman cross—who is this man, who after all that still cries out, 'Forgive them'?

"Furthermore," he continued, "years before, this man Jesus had taught his friends that they must 'love your enemies, pray for those who persecute you'—and then as he was being murdered, he did it. He loved his enemies. He prayed for them."

THE OPPOSITE OF ME

I wasn't a Christian. But I was impressed by this one detail from this man's life. I was really struck by the way that what Jesus had taught was the way Jesus had lived—that there was an exact correlation between his life and his lips. And that struck me because, as a teenager, I was for the first time confronted by my own hypocrisy—by the truth that what I said was right was very different from the way I then lived.

I'd found out that I was a hypocrite through my decision—and this is fairly embarrassing—to keep a diary. Because I was such a great guy who was clearly destined for greatness, I felt that obviously I owed it to the world to record my life. So I kept this diary and I found out that I was a hypocrite. For example, I would call for world peace, and yet never laid aside the weapons of sarcasm and malice that I used in my own self-defence. I would lament world hunger, and yet asked my parents for a bigger allowance. I talked a good game but I didn't live it.

That's what is amazing about the man at the centre of this picture. He is the opposite of me. He is the opposite of so many of our leaders who sooner or later prove incapable of living up to their own standards. They may be leading other people but they cannot lead themselves. Jesus is *different*. He hung there and he said, *This is what I taught and this is what I will do. God, forgive them. God, I want the best for them even as they do their worst to me.*

I found that kind of character absolutely compelling. And I'm not the only one. Take Mitsuo Fuchida. He was the man who led the Japanese assault on Pearl Harbor in 1941—the unprovoked attack on the USA that led four years later to two atomic bombs being dropped on his own country. By the end of the war he was a disillusioned and broken man; and then he read Luke's Gospel—the historical biography of this man Jesus, from which comes the picture we're looking at through this book.

And the turning point in Fuchida's life was this line—"Father, forgive them, for they do not know what they are doing". He became a follower of the man who had said it. The man who had proudly, mercilessly, bombed the US fleet now spent his life telling others to take Jesus, and the forgiveness he spoke of, seriously.

TOO GOOD TO BE TRUE?

I don't know what you make of someone whose teaching inspires unselfishness and integrity, and who then lives it out. I think there are two options: he's truly good, or he's too good to be true. Which is it? Well, Luke isn't writing a fairy story. Here's how he begins his Gospel:

Many have undertaken to draw up an account of the things that have been fulfilled among us, just as they were handed down to us by those who from the first were eye witnesses and servants of the word. With this in mind, since I myself have carefully investigated everything from the beginning, I too decided to write an orderly account for you, most excellent Theophilus, so that you may know the certainty of the things you have been taught. (Luke 1 v 1-4)

He's claiming to be writing history—a record of evidence based on a careful investigation of what eyewitnesses saw and heard. After all, if Luke had been writing fiction, he wouldn't have tried to convince you to believe that a man who was rejected by everyone who mattered and who died a criminal's death on a cross is worth your time and attention.

And that's the tragedy here. This most compelling of men, this man free of hypocrisy and full of integrity, is being killed. We see his love here, but we see it as we witness his death. It's a tragedy—as the note on Jesus at the museum exhibition in London's Millennium Dome put it, "Jesus died tragically young".

LOOK CLOSER

Except... look a little closer at the image, and we see it was no tragic accident. In fact, it was a predicted plan.

As Jesus prayed for forgiveness, the soldiers were playing for his clothes: "And they divided up his clothes by casting lots" (Luke 23 v 34). Jesus' robe was presumably seamless, and so, rather than rip it up, the soldiers gambled for it by casting lots—throwing dice—to see who would win it. And this seemingly insignificant detail in the scene is crucial to understanding it, because a thousand years earlier, a song had been written by a king of Israel, about suffering as Israel's king:

Dogs surround me,
a pack of villains encircles me;
they pierce my hands and my feet.
All my bones are on display;
people stare and gloat over me.
They divide my clothes among them
and cast lots for my garment. (Psalm 22 v 16-18)

These are words written 1,000 years before Jesus was nailed to a cross. Yet they predict not only the practice of crucifixion long before the Phoenicians introduced it and the Romans perfected it, but also the particular circumstances of Jesus' death before a gloating crowd, watching soldiers cast lots to gamble for his garment. It could of course be a huge coincidence; or it could point to this event having been predicted beforehand because it was planned beforehand.

And the details keep coming. So next…

The soldiers also came up and mocked him. They
offered him wine vinegar. (Luke 23 v 36)

And again, around a thousand years earlier, an event was foretold in which a king in Israel would see his enemies "put gall in my food and [give] me vinegar for my thirst" (Psalm 69 v 21).

So in this scene we're seeing not only Jesus'

character, but his identity—not only what he was like, but who he was. During his life, and even when on trial for his life, Jesus had not only claimed to be a great teacher, but a divine figure. He had said he was God himself, who had come to rule his people in fulfilment of the promises made to God's people centuries before—the King to rule all kings, the Messiah. Through the centuries, God had caused many promises and predictions to be written down in what we call the Old Testament. And the night before his death, Jesus told his friends that he saw himself as the one in whom all those plans came together:

> It is written: "And he was numbered with the trans-
> gressors"; and I tell you that this must be fulfilled
> in me. Yes, what is written about me is reaching its
> fulfilment. (Luke 22 v 37)

Think about that. Jesus isn't saying, *I'm going to die because my enemies are going to get the better of me.* He's saying, *I'm going to die because it's part of a greater plan, a plan made and explained by God. I'm not dying because I'm not the Messiah. I'm dying precisely because I am.*

Not that anybody gave that idea much credit at the time—Jesus was being executed, and surely all-powerful kings don't go in for being crucified. So they mock him:

> He saved others; let him save himself if he is God's
> Messiah, the Chosen One. (Luke 23 v 35)

MY MOTHER AND THE POP SINGER

It's very easy to miss someone's real identity. A few years before she died, my mother met the singer Chris De Burgh, of *Lady in Red* fame, at a wedding in Ireland. My mum knew nothing about 80s pop music.

She said to him, "What do you do?"

He said, "I'm a singer."

She said, "Are you a tenor or a bass?"

And he said, "Actually I'm a popular singer."

To which she said, "Well, that must be quite hard financially. Do you have to have a day job? Does your wife work? How do you cope?"

And he replied, "Well, it's nice of you to ask, but actually my records pay for it."

She said, "I'm thrilled, I'm thrilled."

She came back to England and she said to me, "I was talking to a bloke, a singer, called Hamburger or Deberger" and I said, "Was it Chris De Burgh?" I found a picture of him and she said, "That's him!"

I said, "He's worth tens of millions". And her response? "Well, I'm glad to hear it, because he looks undernourished." That reply explains why I have always been two stone overweight.

My mother had no idea who he was; no idea what he was worth; no idea of his fame or identity. Her ignorance made me laugh, and I imagine Chris De Burgh enjoyed it too. Of course, my mother not recognising that man didn't really matter—but it does matter if people don't recognise God when he is right in front of them.

And that's what is going on here. These people see an object of mockery, or at best a human tragedy. What they don't see is divinity. *But they should.* After all, it's one thing to set out in your life to fulfil a bunch of centuries-old prophecies about a future king. But it's impossible to make sure they are fulfilled when your hands and feet are nailed to a cross. You can't rig hardened soldiers casting lots for your clothing. You can't organise your enemies giving you wine vinegar as they mock you.

And you can't do the things Jesus had done before he hung on that cross, either. This was a man who had gone up to a paralysed man and said, "Get up and walk" and he had—his muscles and tendons and bones had been knitted together, and in front of the watching crowds he'd got up and walked away. A man who had said, "Be clean" to a man suffering a skin disease that left his nerves shot and meant he was shunned by society—a "leper"—and he was healed, instantly. A man who had been in a boat during a massive storm with some experienced fishermen who were convinced they were about to be drowned, and he'd calmly said to the wind and waves, "Be still!" and they went calm and flat. A man who had been led by a dead 12-year-old's parents into her room, with her corpse stretched out on her bed, and he'd said, "Little girl, I say to you, get up"—and she'd got up.

IMPOSSIBLE

Now all that sounds far-fetched. In fact, let's be clear—it's impossible. No man can do such things. But the One who created humanity could. And that's the point. These are astonishing miracles. But if Jesus was God himself, living in his own creation as a man, the divine Master breaking into human history, isn't this what you'd expect to see? This man—this man who prays for his enemies, who fulfils ancient predictions, and who controls the weather and has power over sickness—he's not just truly good. He's truly God.

One man who knew Jesus for years, who saw all that he did and said, and who stood at the foot of his cross as he died, put it this way:

> *No one has ever seen God, but the one and only Son, who is himself God and is in the closest relationship with the Father, has made him known ... We have seen his glory, the glory of the one and only Son, who came from the Father. (John 1 v 18, 14)*

This man, John, had seen the glory—the "godness"—of God. He'd seen it in a human—a human who was the Son of God, who had lived eternally with his Father and the Spirit. Jesus is uniquely able to show us who God is. And he shows us that, mysteriously, God is one God and three Persons—Father, Son and Spirit.

This is a view of God that is hard to get your head around. But that's OK, because a God whom we could get our heads around completely would be a pretty small, tame kind of "God". And it's wonderful, because it means that the central reality of existence is not power, or possessions, or pointlessness, but a being who is within himself all about relationship, friendship, love and trust. The reality of who the real God is is mind-boggling; and it's brilliant; it's glorious. And the world glimpsed this glory as God the Son walked on its surface, breathed its air, spoke and slept and laughed and cried and, yes, died.

GOD'S SELF PORTRAIT

So any God-given image of God—any self-portrait that sums him up—will have Jesus at the centre of it. God shows us himself by himself coming into the world.

That may be a surprise to you—that Jesus cannot be dismissed as a fake, or cannot be vaguely ignored as a good man, a tragic figure or a master teacher— because the claims he made and the things he did mean you must deal with him not only as a man but as God.

But this should be of greater shock to you—that God came, and *God chose to die*. The picture that reveals him most clearly is not one of him touching that leper, or standing up on that boat, or in that dead girl's room. It is the picture of him being brutally executed. If you want to see God, you must see Jesus. And you must see him bleeding and dying on a cross. Talking about his death, Jesus himself said, "The hour has come for [me] to be glorified" (John 12 v 23). The glory, the "godness", of God is captured at the cross.

When you look at Jesus hanging there, what kind of God do you see revealed? You see a God of integrity, who commands nothing he does not do himself; and a God of intentionality, who planned the worst moment of his own life, who walked resolutely towards his own execution.

And when you look at him there, in his self-portrait at his execution, the question has to be: *Why?*

⌜3⌝

WELCOME

I want you to know that the only reason I watched the film *Titanic* starring Leonardo Di Caprio and Kate Winslet was because I had been asked to look after my two younger cousins, both young teenagers, and I thought if I put it on for them I could get some sleep while they watched it.

But I didn't go to sleep, because I was gripped— not by the romance of the Leonardo Di Caprio-Kate Winslet love story, but by knowing the boat would sink and then watching the reaction to the boat start-ing to sink. There's one scene I've never forgotten. It comes just after the captain, the engineer and the owner have realised that, having struck the iceberg, in a few hours the ship will sink. Everything will be at the bottom of the ocean.

And at that point the director, James Cameron, takes us round the boat, and it's a scene of jollity and grandeur. The first-class passengers do not have a care in the world. They have no idea about the reality. The ship's going to sink, but it's a scene of the pinnacle of luxury. The chandeliers are resplendent, the wide curved staircase is regal, everything glitters and is furnished in gold leaf, the drinks are free, people are dripping with jewels.

And if you'd stepped onto the boat and done a survey of these people about how life was going, what would they have said? "We're rich, we're happy, we're on the Titanic, we haven't a care in the world." Not even God could sink this boat, someone had said as it left Southampton for its maiden voyage across the Atlantic. But all it had taken in fact was a single iceberg; and knowing the reality of the situation, you don't feel envy for these rich, happy people, but rather pity. They're blind to the fact that in an hour or so, everything will change. The ship is holed, it will sink, and there are not enough lifeboats. More than 1,500 lives are about to end, and the finest jewels and clothes won't help at all.

As the shipbuilder put it to Kate Winslet—sorry, to Rose—in one of those helpfully coincidental meetings that happen in films in order to make sure the dimmest possible member of the cinema audience has grasped what is going on, "The ship will sink."

"You're certain?" asks Rose.

"Yes," he replies. "In an hour or so, all of this will be at the bottom of the Atlantic."

The truth, in reality just as in the film, was that the ship would sink. And for many, many people, their future was a long, lingering descent into death in icy waters.

WHAT DO YOU DO WITH DEATH?

Here's the issue. You'll never understand what Jesus was doing hanging on the cross, and why God would have *planned* for that to happen to his own Son, unless you begin to understand that we are all in a *Titanic* situation. I told you about Emma, the girl whose looks got me to go to church and hear of a man who prayed for forgiveness for his enemies as they murdered him. I was impressed by him. But a year later, I was no longer merely impressed by him: I needed him. During the summer holidays, we had a phone call to tell us the news that rocked everything: my uncle, my godfather, had died. He'd been walking along a cliff path, he'd tried to hop over a fallen tree, and he'd slipped, fallen, and died.

And I realised at that moment: people die. It's obvious, isn't it? But no one—and I mean no one, in my family, at school, no friend or teacher, no one— had ever spoken to me about death. It happens to everyone, and yet no one really talks about it. We do our best to live as though we're not heading for it.

Here's what we tend to do about death in the West. We choose one of three options. First, we disengage from it. We just pretend it's not there. Near where I live, there's a great playground. It's where I take the kids when I—sorry, they—want a go on the slide. For centuries it was a cemetery, right in the middle of the community. But now they've moved the cemetery miles away, behind a high wall, away from sight, and they've put a playground in instead. It's symbolic of what we do with death as a culture. We hide it. We pretend it won't happen, though painful personal experience tells us that it does and it will. We disengage.

Second, we distort it. So one of the most popular poems at British funerals is this one, by Henry Scott Holland. He was a pastor, and he intended the main point to come in the second verse, where he talks of how death can be a doorway to life beyond. But usually, only the first verse is read or remembered:

Death is nothing at all.
I have only slipped away to the next room.
I am I and you are you.
Whatever we were to each other,
That, we still are.

Stop there, and the point is completely changed from Holland's intention. The basic message becomes

Death is nothing. How unrealistic. Try telling that to the husband whose wife dies after 40 years of marriage—and years later he is still reaching over to her side of the bed only to remember that there's no one there, and the wave of grief hits him all over again. Try telling that to the mother who watches her son slip away from her.

So we disengage from death, or we distort what death is, but then every now and then we have to confront the reality… and we start to despair about death—because death mocks all our achievements and accumulations. John-Paul Sartre, the twentieth-century philosopher, who was commendably unafraid of looking at the reality of death and drawing the logical conclusions of his atheism, wrote:

> *Nothing happens while you live. The scenery changes, people come in and go out, that's all. There are no beginnings. Days are tacked on to days without rhyme or reason, an interminable monotonous addition …*
> *There is nothing, no reason for existing.*

DEALING WITH IT

God does not ignore the reality of death. It's very striking that this most personal of pictures of him involves death—it has death at its heart. On that day, in that place, three men did not have the option of ignoring death—of disengaging from it. Death was very real to them. It was hours away, and unlike the first-class Titanic passengers they had nails in their hands and legs, forcing them to confront it.

And the two men either side of Jesus dealt with death very differently:

> *One of the criminals who hung there hurled insults at him: "Aren't you the Messiah? Save yourself and us!"*

> *But the other criminal rebuked him. "Don't you fear God," he said, "since you are under the same sentence? We are punished justly, for we are getting what our deeds deserve. But this man has done nothing wrong."*

> *Then he said, "Jesus, remember me when you come into your kingdom." (Luke 23 v 39-42)*

Both men are looking death in the face. And one rages against it. He goes into the night furious— furious with Jesus. He goes as the poet Dylan Thomas recommends we all go:

> *Do not go gentle into that good night,*
> *Old age should burn and rave at close of day;*
> *Rage, rage against the dying of the light.*

But the other man rebukes his raging friend. Everyone is sneering at Jesus—except him. He sees Jesus totally differently. So he warns the other criminal to "fear God" instead of raging at him. Somehow he realises that to criticise Jesus is to criticise God, to mock Jesus is to mock God, and that's a foolish thing to do when you're hours from eternity.

After all, he knows he's done wrong. He knows he's receiving his rightful punishment. "We are getting what our deeds deserve," he says. He doesn't blame bad luck, bad laws, bad parents or a bad background. *No*, he says, *I did it, I was wrong, and I deserve to be here.* You don't meet many people that honest about their own flaws.

And so he doesn't rage against Jesus—but neither is he resigned to his fate. Instead, he has a request to make:

Jesus, remember me when you come into your kingdom.

It's not that he just wants Jesus to think of him—*Ah, I remember that guy on the cross next to me as I died.* No, he wants Jesus to act for him—to bring him into the kingdom. That's the kind of "remembering" he's asking for. If a wife says, "Remember it's our anniversary next week", she is not expecting her husband merely not to forget that fact, but to do something about that fact— to book the table or buy the flowers. And this man wants Jesus to act for him once Jesus has reached his kingdom beyond death, an eternal place with a perfect Ruler, without flaws and beyond decay. He wants Jesus to remember him. To welcome him.

REMEMBER ME

So this man hangs the weight of his eternal future on Jesus. As he hangs there, and he looks across, he doesn't see a mere northern carpenter from the nothing town of Nazareth, who got himself in the wrong place at the wrong time. He sees his God, who came from heaven and who planned to get himself there at that exact time. He offers nothing, but he asks for everything. He asks the King of the world beyond death to "remember" him:

Please don't forget me. I don't deserve anything from you. I make no excuses. I'm just asking you to welcome me when you come into your kingdom.

This, by the way, is what faith is. It is reaching out and saying, *I'm not bringing anything. I'm just asking you, and trusting you. Please remember me.*

The problem is who is asking the question, and who he's asking it to. This is a man whose crimes Luke doesn't detail—but they have brought him to his execution. And he is asking for eternal peace from another man who has nails through his hands and his feet, and whose every breath, let alone every word, brings searing pain.

So what should Jesus say?

Not a chance, you bigot. You're a terrorist, a murderer and a thief. You think God would have you anywhere near him in his perfect world? You understand I'm in charge of that place, and yet you think that I'd let a man like you into it?

Or:

My dear friend, I wish I could help. But don't pray to me—I'm a man like you, and there's nothing I can do. I know nothing about what lies beyond this cross, this death. I'm sorry.

Or:

I'm glad you've worked it out. Now you need to get yourself off this cross, and go and make up for all the wrong you've done, and make sure you do good things every day, and then if you do that for decades, it's possible that I might consider it enough to let you in.

No.

Truly I tell you, today you will be with me in paradise.
                                                        (Luke 23 v 43)

No conditions. No qualifications. No delays. This is God, inviting a failure to join him in eternity, to enjoy eternity. That's Jesus' promise. *Yes, there is a place in my kingdom for you. I will never forget you. I promise. By the end of the day, you'll be dead, and you'll be more alive than ever before.*

THE "EARN IT" BURDEN

I started this chapter with a film—I'm going to finish with one too. *Saving Private Ryan* is a Second World War film about a young man called James Ryan who is fighting in the US Army in France in 1944 when his mother learns on a single day that his three older brothers have been killed. A US General orders that this fourth son is to be rescued and returned home so that his mother won't lose him too. So Tom Hanks and his squad of seven men go to find him and rescue him, and they succeed—but most, including Tom Hanks, die in the operation. And at the end of the film as Tom Hanks lies dying, he says to James Ryan:

> *James, earn this. Earn it.*

And those are his last words.

Then the film flicks forward 50 years, and James Ryan is an old man, back in northern France, at the grave of Tom Hanks. And as he kneels by the grave he weeps and says:

> *Every day I've thought about what you said… I've tried to live my life the best I could. I hope that was enough. I hope that at least in your eyes, I've earned what all of you have done for me.*

And he turns to his wife and rather desperately he says:

> *Tell me I have led a good life. Tell me I'm a good man.*

Right through his life, those words "earn it, earn it" have rung in his ears. He's lived under that burden. Every day he's had to try to deserve what men had died to give him.

God did not hang on the cross to tell us to earn life. He did not tell the criminal next to him that he'd need to offer something to him, some goodness or morality or achievement. He just promised him a place in his kingdom that he could never deserve.

He's the God of second chances, of last chances, of only chances. He's the God who sends a lifeboat to the sinking ship, so that the icy waters of death need not be the end, but instead a welcome onto the firm, dry ground of his kingdom can be the future. He's the God who *is* the lifeboat.

This is God. He's the God who we see hanging on a cross to offer a welcome into heaven. He does not say, *You must earn it*. He says, *I will give it*.

And so here is what a Christian is. It is someone who has asked for a place in heaven, and who knows they need not and could never earn it—it would never be enough—but that they have been given it. Christianity is not about what you earn. It's about what you're given.

And so ultimately it doesn't matter whether you have lived a good life, or have lived the opposite; it doesn't matter whether you have lived a full life, or the opposite. Only Jesus can offer life beyond death, and Jesus does offer that life—to everyone. He enables us to look at death without despair, because he gives us a way to look through death to life with him beyond it. Even that criminal. Even you. Even me.

⌜4⌟
JUSTICE

I f after reading the last chapter you have a problem with the idea that Jesus welcomed a convicted criminal, a murderous terrorist, into his kingdom with open arms, then you're in good company.

God does, too.

Our problem with a terrorist being allowed to enjoy perfection for eternity—whether 2,000 years ago or today—is due to our inbuilt sense of justice. Justice is the impulse that demands people get what they deserve. It's why we feel angry when a murder is committed and the murderer is never caught. It's why our hearts go out to those who are wrongfully imprisoned for a crime they didn't commit, while the guilty person walks around free. It's why we feel dissatisfied that Hitler and Stalin cheated justice by dying before they were ever brought to trial and made to answer for killing so many people.

We want there to be justice. And if there is a God, we want him to bring justice. We don't want him to wink at evil or smile weakly at terror. We want it to matter to him, and we want him to do something about it.

The cross says: *He does, he has, and he will.* And that is both satisfying for us, and terrifying for us.

GOD CARES

The King and the criminal finished their conversation at "about noon" (v 44): "and darkness came over the whole land until three in the afternoon". A historian who lived north of Israel, Thallus, recorded this darkness. He thought it was an eclipse, but eclipses only last five or six minutes rather than three hours—and it was a full moon, and so the moon was in completely the wrong place for an eclipse to occur. This was a supernatural occurrence. This was God intervening to bring darkness.

Every member of Israel standing near those three crosses would have known what supernatural darkness represented. It meant God's anger; it heralded God's justice. He had promised that a sign that his justice was coming was that…

> *I will make the sun go down at noon and darken the earth in broad daylight. (Amos 8 v 9)*

This isn't a wild, uncontrolled anger of the kind that all too often we see around us and even within us—God's anger is his settled, controlled personal hostility to evil. God does care what happens in his world.

I take solace in that. I've been the victim of real malice on a couple of occasions, and I like knowing that that really matters to the real God as well as to me. But unlike me, he has the power to do something about that malice. If you have been the victim of evil, of sin, then this darkness tells you that God does care and God will act. What I do to you matters to God and what you do to me matters to God.

Jesus himself pictured God's justice in terms of darkness. He described the place beyond the borders of his kingdom as being, "outside, [in] the darkness, where there will be weeping and gnashing of teeth" (Matthew 25 v 30). So the darkness above the cross does not just tell you that God's justice will come, but what God's judgment is. Because God cares about what goes on in his world, he will shut out of his world those who do evil in his world. Imagine a life spent in constant darkness, with no light whatsoever, and no hope of ever having any. A life beyond death without hope, or friendship, or anything to look at or look forward to, for ever, with only tears and regret for company. It's a place Jesus called "hell". It's the place of the judgment of God on those who choose to use the light of the sun that he made to treat with contempt the world and the people he has made.

NOT ONLY VICTIMS

This is great news for us when we suffer; but it is also very worrying for us because we are all sinners. We are not only victims of sin; we are practitioners of it too. But sin is a very unpopular idea in our society. 45 years ago, a psychologist, Karl Menninger, summed it up very well as he traced how the notion of evil has slipped from being sin against God for which you are to blame, to being crime against other people for which you are still to blame, to being a sickness or a weakness for which you are not at fault:

> *Disease and treatment have been the watchwords of the day and little is said about selfishness or guilt … and certainly no one talks about sin!*

If my problem is psychological, then what I need is a good therapist. But the darkness over the cross warns me that my real problem is that I am a sinner. I am a rebel against God—I try to climb into his place and sit on his throne.

I heard not long ago of a schoolgirl who got drunk and then gave three friends a lift home. And before she got into the car, she stood by her door with her keys and said, "My car, my rules". She felt she had the right to decide how she drove and when she drove because it was her car. The car never got home. She survived the crash unscathed, but one of her passengers was killed and the other two were disabled.

It could be the slogan for our lives: *My life, my rules.* We will decide how we live. Our problem is not so much that we are rule-breakers but that we're rule-makers. And the rules we make are catastrophic for those around us—sometimes in ways we can see and sometimes in ways we can't. I know that I can be selfishly hurtful, even to those I love most. I can sometimes get so angry that I could punch people. I allow my mind to wander towards lust. I am often driven by a desire for others to think I am great, so I tell lies, exaggerate stories or amend the truth to make myself look good, even if it means taking the credit from someone who deserves it.

You're probably not a drunk-driver—but in your more honest moments, you'll be aware that you are sometimes selfish, or unthoughtful, or even deliberately nasty. The self-promoting conversation that subtly criticises someone else. The mocking tone that crushes someone else. The thoughtless inaction that abandons someone else. You decide what to think and do and say, and at times—too many times—those decisions are made at the expense of others.

Not only that, but our rule-making is catastrophic for *us*, too—because it means we deserve only to be put "outside, into the darkness, where there will be weeping and gnashing of teeth". We say, *My life, my rules,* and God says, *Fine, if you want me out the picture, you will discover what it means to live without me, separated from me, without light, for ever.* That's his judgment. That's his justice.

TEARING THE CURTAIN

Actually, those alive in Jesus' time and place could never forget that they faced separation from God, both in this life and beyond death. The largest building in Jerusalem, a few hundred yards from where the criminals were crucified, was the temple, the building God had told people to build. And the temple acted as a huge visual aid. In the temple, an 80-foot-high curtain hung. It was about as thick as a man's hand, embroidered with purple and gold, and on one side was the area people could go into, and on the other was the space—the only space in the world—where God was present in all his power and perfection.

And so this curtain was hanging there to say, *It is impossible for you to come into God's presence and enjoy life in his kingdom. You can't come through here and survive—you'd face death and darkness. Your sin keeps you out.* On one side was the world, operating according to the principle *My life, my rules*; on the other was God's place, where he set the rules and he gave life. And in between was this massive curtain, like a spiritual no-entry sign hung on an electric fence.

Now picture this huge, thick, physically and spiritually impenetrable curtain. And as the darkness descended, "the curtain of the temple was torn in two". God did what no human could do. He ripped up the no-entry sign. The presence of God is opened up, the problem of our sin is dealt with, a criminal can be welcomed into the kingdom, the darkness lifts… and yet no one has died.

No one, except the King of that kingdom. No one, except the Son of God:

> *The curtain of the temple was torn in two. Jesus called out with a loud voice, "Father, into your hands I commit my spirit." When he had said this, he breathed his last. (Luke 23 v 45-46)*

Even the two criminals either side of Jesus lived for hours after the darkness lifted. The only person who died in the darkness of God's judgment was… God. The only person who died in order to open up the way to God's presence was… God.

And that's the point. That's why he hung there. That's why he ignored all the mocking calls to climb off the cross. He hung there not because he had to, but because he chose to.

SHATTERED

Before I was married, I cycled around London for 14 years without ever wearing a cycle helmet. But after six months of increasingly pointed requests, Lucy convinced me to wear one. That same year, I was on my bike, cycling along normally, when I crashed. My front wheel jammed between the bars of a road drain. The bike stopped dead, I flew over the handle bars, and I hit the tarmac head first. My helmet shattered.

900 people a year die from cycling accidents in the US (and over 100 in the UK). 60% of those are from head injuries. Without that helmet, there is absolutely no way that I would not have added one more to the numbers. I would have been dead in minutes. But I was wearing the helmet. It got smashed to pieces, but I just stood up and I was fine, to the shock of passers-by who had seen me not so much head-butt but torpedo the road. If it weren't for Lucy telling me to wear the helmet, I'd have been dead. Because of the cycle helmet, I was alive.

Cycle helmets are designed for exactly this event. They are hard on the outside, to spread the impact over the whole helmet as you hit the ground; and they have a soft liner underneath, to absorb the energy of the impact so that it's not transmitted to your head. But in order to absorb that impact, the helmet has to shatter. So when I stood up from my crash, my helmet was as destroyed as my head would have been had I not been wearing it.

My helmet saved my life because it took the full force, was destroyed by it, and in doing so it protected me. And that is a small and inadequate picture of what Jesus did on the cross. Here was God, taking his own justice, bearing his own anger, taking into himself the darkness that should be mine. All my rebellion against God that brings down his anger, Jesus took the full force of it. And he was shattered for me as he died. He breathed his last instead of me. He experienced the darkness as he died so that the criminal dying next to him would not have to endure it after he died.

Where I live in London, even amid the skyscrapers there is one very prominent building on the skyline. It's the Old Bailey, the courts that are the home of British justice. And on the roof is the golden statue of Lady Justice; there she stands, blindfolded, for she is fair, not showing favouritsm. In one hand are the scales of justice, and in the other is the sword of justice. And the message is clear: whoever you are and whatever you think, if you are found wanting in the scales, the sword must fall. But then if you track your gaze along from the Old Bailey, you see the roofline of St Paul's Cathedral. And there stands a golden cross. And that tells me that on the cross God's justice came, but it came on his Son. The sword fell on him rather than me.

What kind of God dies on a cross? One who cares about justice for the people he has made. The cross is a glimpse of the punishment facing everyone who hurts others as they live with a *"My life, my rules"* attitude.

But of course that's not all. God died on a cross because he cares about the eternal lives of the people he has made. On the cross, God punished God. God the Son took the darkness of separation from his Father in himself so that people don't need to bear it for themselves.

The God we see on the cross does not merely tell us to wear the only helmet that will protect us from the impact of his judgment. He does not merely provide the helmet. He *is* the helmet. Our sin shattered him—and as he was shattered, he saved us.

⌜5⌝
PEACE

That picture should be the end of the story. A dead man, killed on a cross, buried in a tomb. It should be the end of the story.

It wasn't.

> On the first day of the week, very early in the morning, the women took the spices they had prepared and went to the tomb. They found the stone rolled away from the tomb, but when they entered, they did not find the body of the Lord Jesus. While they were wondering about this, suddenly two men in clothes that gleamed like lightning stood beside them. In their fright the women bowed down with their faces to the ground, but the men said to them, "Why do you look for the living among the dead? He is not here; he has risen! Remember how he told you, while

he was still with you in Galilee: 'The Son of Man must be delivered over to the hands of sinners, be crucified and on the third day be raised again.'" Then they remembered his words.

When they came back from the tomb, they told all these things to the Eleven and to all the others. It was Mary Magdalene, Joanna, Mary the mother of James, and the others with them who told this to the apostles. But they did not believe the women, because their words seemed to them like nonsense.

(Luke 24 v 1-11)

Later that day, in the evening, in a locked room in Jerusalem, where a group of Jesus' friends had gathered...

Jesus himself stood among them and said to them, "Peace be with you."

They were startled and frightened, thinking they saw a ghost. He said to them, "Why are you troubled, and why do doubts rise in your minds? Look at my hands and my feet. It is I myself! Touch me and see; a ghost does not have flesh and bones, as you see I have."

When he had said this, he showed them his hands and feet. And while they still did not believe it because of joy and amazement, he asked them, "Do

CAPTURING GOD

you have anything here to eat?" They gave him a piece of broiled fish, and he took it and ate it in their presence.

He said to them, "This is what I told you while I was still with you: everything must be fulfilled that is written about me in the Law of Moses, the Prophets and the Psalms."

Then he opened their minds so they could understand the Scriptures. He told them, "This is what is written: the Messiah will suffer and rise from the dead on the third day, and repentance for the forgiveness of sins will be preached in his name to all nations, beginning at Jerusalem. You are witnesses of these things. I am going to send you what my Father has promised; but stay in the city until you have been clothed with power from on high." (Luke 24 v 36-49)

HARD TO BELIEVE

It's hard to believe a man rose from the dead. And the Bible doesn't ask you to shut your eyes and make a leap of faith. Instead, it encourages you to open your eyes, look at the evidence, and make a step of faith.

The women who went to that tomb that morning and the people who were gathered in that room that evening were not stupid. They knew dead people didn't rise. That's why the women were taking spices with them, to rub on the corpse they knew they would find, to stop it smelling as it decomposed. That's why Jesus' eleven closest friends, and those they were with, knew the resurrection was "nonsense". They knew that if there were any other explanation, it was probably the correct one.

And so Jesus gave them, and gives us, evidence—proof after proof that it's really him, really risen. Just in this one episode in that room, he appeared to them. He spoke to them. He pointed to the nail-marks in his hands and feet. He invited them to touch him to check. He ate something. And that's just this one occasion. Jesus was seen and spoken to on numerous occasions, sometimes by small groups, and at least once by a gathering of hundreds.

The strange truth is that to believe in the resurrection is not to follow a preconception or prejudice—it is to follow the historical evidence. A question worth asking is: Is there a better historical explanation for the incontestable events of the first Easter Sunday—an empty tomb, joy-filled friends, frequent sightings? (If you want to think more about this, one great book to read is *The Case for Easter* by Lee Strobel, a journalist who as an atheist set out to disprove Christianity, and found himself unwillingly convinced by it instead.)

PEACE OFFER

Jesus didn't only appear. That alone would have established the truth of the resurrection. He also spoke. He wanted to explain the implications of his resurrection.

Here were his first words to these friends who had run away when he was arrested, and who thought it was nonsense when he rose:

Peace be with you. (Luke 24 v 36)

Jesus came to offer peace with God—to declare peace with God to anyone who asks him for it. His whole life, and supremely his death and resurrection, were designed to bring peace to a humanity that has said to God, *Get out. My life, my rules.*

By "peace", Jesus doesn't mean some wishy-washy, vague feeling that everything's OK, that refuses to engage with reality. He means the kind of peace that matters—a peace that replaces conflict, that changes everything, that is worth celebrating. A relationship restored. A battle over. The kind of peace that sends people onto the streets after a war has ended.

To live at peace is a wonderful thing. After all, almost all of us want to be at peace with others. We don't like feeling that someone else thinks badly of us—that we have enemies. And the more impor-tant someone is to us, the more we need peace with them. When (new helmet firmly on head) I annoy a car driver on my bike, and he shouts at me, it upsets me for a moment, but not for long. When I say something that hurts my wife, so that we're not at peace, that dominates my day and colours all my feelings.

The most important relationship you have is with God. He is your Creator and your Sustainer—the one who holds you in the palm of his hand. He is the almighty planet-making, star-controlling, universe-ruling God. You do not want to be out of peace with him. You do not want to stay at war with him. You do not want to face him one day as his enemy, with darkness stretching ahead.

So it is a great relief that we can hear Jesus say, "Peace be with you". Battle over. Relationship restored.

If you realise this, then everything changes. You can face the world with confidence—you're at peace with the One who owns the place! You can be honest with yourself about yourself. When you mess up—when you sin—you don't need to try to ignore it, or seek to hide it, or work to excuse it. You can front up, and accept you're wrong and flawed, but know that in Jesus you're nevertheless at peace with God.

You don't need to strive to gain peace with God, to earn peace with God, to maintain your peace with God. You don't need to do anything. You just need to look to the risen Jesus and hear him say to you, "Peace be with you". You can go out into your day knowing that you have, and can't lose, the most important peace there is. You're not arrogant about your achievements, because you needed Jesus to win you and give you peace with God. You're not crushed by your failings, because you know it's Jesus who gives you peace with God.

CLOTHED WITH POWER

There's more. Jesus also promised the men and women gathered in that room on the evening of the first Easter Sunday that they would be "clothed with power from on high". Jesus was talking about the Holy Spirit—God himself. Through coming as Jesus, God had been present with people—and soon, through sending his Spirit after the risen Jesus had returned to heaven, he would remain present with people. And he still is.

So the power that made a paralysed man walk… that healed a leper… that controlled a storm… that raised a dead girl and a crucified man… that power is with people because God comes powerfully to be with people. It means that people can change in ways they never thought they could. People can have courage in ways that defy explanation. People can commit to following a God who was unpopular when he walked on earth and is unpopular still today.

To hear Jesus say to you "Peace be with you" is wonderfully liberating. To know Jesus is powerfully with you is wonderfully reassuring. Here is God—the God of the cross, and the God who lives beyond the cross—the God who cannot be beaten by death and who beckons us from beyond death and says, *Here's my offer—my peace with you, and my power in you.*

⌜6⌝

FINDING YOURSELF

Let me take you back to this picture of God hanging on a cross, bleeding and dying—because there's one more surprising aspect to it.

You're in it.

As you pictured the scene at the start of this book, you will have imagined not only the man hanging on the middle cross, or the two criminals crucified on his right and his left, but three groups of other people too. In fact, although this image is focused on the figure in the centre—on Jesus—it's crowded with others.

And all of them react to the cross in different ways. All of them see something as they look at this man. But all of them see very different things. It's as though Luke is saying, *Who are you in this scene? What do you see as you look at this image?*

THE SOLDIERS, THE RULERS AND THE CROWD

First, there are the soldiers. It's their job to carry out the execution—and they do:

> *They crucified him there, along with the criminals …*
> *and they divided up his clothes by casting lots.*
>
> *(Luke 23 v 33-34)*

For these men, the main legacy of the cross is Jesus' clothes. They're absorbed in doing their job, and they do it very well. They have time for a little mockery, offering this so-called king wine vinegar as he hangs there, but mainly for them it's a job, with perks. In their desire for material things, they miss what is going on right in front of their eyes.

Many of us go through life doing our duty. We work hard; we pay the bills; we provide for ourselves and those close to us. And the day-to-day busyness of our intense lives—the daily chase to make sure we and our loved ones have enough—blinds us to the true significance of the cross. God hangs his picture on the wall and says *Here I am*, but we are too busy with life and too absorbed with the here-and-now to notice it.

Second, there are the "rulers"—those who ran the religious activities of Jerusalem, and who had seen Jesus as such a threat to their view of life and position in society that they'd had him arrested, put on trial facing trumped-up charges, and condemned to death.

> *The rulers … sneered at him. They said, "He saved*
> *others; let him save himself if he is God's Messiah,*
> *the Chosen One." (Luke 23 v 35)*

These religious rulers are convinced that they already know the way to God—and the cross is not a part of that route. They are convinced that they are the ones who get to decide what standards earn God's favour—and submitting to Jesus as Ruler is not a part of that arrangement. For them, the cross is nothing but a demonstration of Jesus' weakness and the emptiness of his claims.

It is often those of us who think of ourselves as spiritual or religious who are the most offended by the cross and who go to the greatest lengths to reject the God who hung on it. We want to consider ourselves as good, moral, and acceptable to God. We want to earn heaven, not to have to be given it. If you think you are good, you don't need God to die for you. God hangs his picture on the wall and says *Here I am*, but we hang our own portrait over it and look to our own efforts to save us.

Third, there is the crowd:

> *When all the people who had gathered to witness this*
> *sight saw what took place, they beat their breasts and*
> *went away. (Luke 23 v 48)*

These people recognised that what had happened

was a tragedy, something worth mourning rather than celebrating—so they "beat their breasts", a cultural way of expressing sadness or regret or even guilt. And then they "went away". The events of that day had shown them, or reminded them, that the world is a broken, unfair place; perhaps some even sensed that the man who had just been murdered was no ordinary man. But they had not realised that the events of that day also provided the solution to the brokenness, and a way to a world beyond death and a life of perfection and fairness.

It's very easy to be moved by what we see at the cross. It's very easy to be struck by what it tells us about life. It's even very easy to realise that there is something special going on here.

And then it's very easy to walk away. God hangs his picture on the wall and says *Here I am*, and we look hard, think hard, and walk away. The cross is interesting, striking, moving—but not life-changing.

THE CENTURION

Those are the three groups. Then there is the one individual Luke shows us standing near the cross. He's a Roman centurion, a hard-bitten military officer, and when Jesus breathed his last…

> *The centurion, seeing what had happened, praised*
> *God and said, "Surely this was a righteous man."*
> *(Luke 23 v 47)*

This man had doubtless fought many campaigns, and seen many men die—but he'd never seen a man die like this. He understood that Jesus was "righteous", or innocent—innocent of making up his claim to be God's Son, God's King, and guilty only of being who he said he was. In other words, the centurion looked hard at the cross and realised that the man on it was telling the truth. He understood that this was God's Son, dying as the fulfilment of God's plan to welcome sinful people into his kingdom beyond death.

YOU

This is where the picture God provides—the image that best captures him—gets very challenging. Because it captures us too. It shows us ourselves. Where do you find yourself in the picture?

Are you like the soldiers, too busy with life to even look at the cross?

Are you like the religious leaders, too sure of your own goodness to need the cross?

Are you like the people, interested in or saddened by, but not *changed* by, what you see at the cross?

Or are you like the centurion? Have you stood looking at the cross as you've read this book and been surprised, perhaps offended, possibly shocked, but ultimately convinced that Jesus is the Son of God, who died for you?

Do you need to say of Jesus, like that army officer: *This man is telling the truth about who he is and what he offers?*

Do you need to say to Jesus, like the condemned criminal,

> *Jesus, my sins deserve the sentence of death and darkness. Jesus, you did nothing wrong, unlike me. Jesus, you are the King. Jesus, please remember me when you come into your kingdom.*

God has offered you one picture of himself that captures his essence. His integrity. His plan. His welcome. His justice. His forgiveness. God is offering you peace with him and power from him.

He's the God who you need, and he's the God who is there. The picture that best sums him up is the one where a man is brutally murdered, in the darkness, on a cross.

Will you look at it? And what will you do with it?

WHAT NEXT?

Thanks for reading this far—I hope you've enjoyed the book and found it thought-provoking. Now you're on the last page, it's worth asking yourself, *What next?*

Maybe you would like to look at Jesus some more before you make your mind up about how to respond to him. If that's you, I'd love you to do two things. First, read a Gospel—why not read the rest of Luke's account of Jesus' life? Second, pray—speak to God and ask him, if he is there, to help you see the reality about who he is and who you are.

There are two other things you could do. Go to a website—christianityexplored.org allows you to keep thinking about Jesus in your own way, at your own pace. Or go on a course: *Christianity Explored* and *Life Explored* are informal ways to hear more, and ask questions, discuss or simply listen. You can find a course near you on that website.

Perhaps, though, you are someone who has said to Jesus yourself those words in italics on the previous page—you've become a Christian. If that's you, that's fantastic! Your life has just changed in a wonderful way. But getting going as a Christian can feel daunting. The best things you can do are to find a church near you that bases all it says and does on the Bible (the same way this book does) and to start speaking to God (praying) and listening to God (reading his word, the Bible). If you'd like a hand with doing any of those, do contact me at: info@thegoodbook.co.uk.

Thanks again for reading. *Rico*

thegoodbook
COMPANY
Opening up the Bible

Thanks for reading this book. We hope you enjoyed it, and found it helpful.

Most people want to find answers to the big questions of life: Who are we? Why are we here? How should we live? But for many valid reasons we are often unable to find the time or the right space to think positively and carefully about them.

Perhaps you have questions that you need an answer for. Perhaps you have met Christians who have seemed unsympathetic or incomprehensible. Or maybe you are someone who has grown up believing, but need help to make things a little clearer.

At The Good Book Company, we're passionate about producing materials that help people of all ages and stages understand the heart of the Christian message, which is found in the pages of the Bible.

Whoever you are, and wherever you are at when it comes to these big questions, we hope we can help. As a publisher we want to help you look at the good book that is the Bible because we're convinced that as we meet the person who stands at its centre—Jesus Christ—we find the clearest answers to our biggest questions.

Visit our website to discover the range of books, videos and other resources we produce, or visit our partner site www.christianityexplored. org for a clear explanation of who Jesus is and why he came.

Thanks again for reading,

Your friends at The Good Book Company

UK & EUROPE
NORTH AMERICA
AUSTRALIA
NEW ZEALAND

thegoodbook.co.uk
thegoodbook.com
thegoodbook.com.au
thegoodbook.co.nz

0333 123 0880
866 244 2165
(02) 6100 4211
(+64) 3 343 2463

WWW.CHRISTIANITYEXPLORED.ORG
Our partner site is a great place for those exploring the Christian faith, with a clear explanation of the good news, powerful testimonies and answers to difficult questions.